SO. S.F. PUBLIC LIBRARY
GRAND AVENUE

G

HOW TO DRAW YOUR OWN SUPERCHARACTERS™

EARL R. PHELPS

HOW TO DRAW YOUR OWN SUPERCHARACTERS™
by Earl R. Phelps

Copyright © 1981, 1986, 1993 by Earl R. Phelps

All rights reserved.
No part of this book may be published
in any form or by any means without
permission in writing from the author.

Published by Phelps Publishing
P.O. Box 22401
Cleveland, Ohio 44122

Printed in the United States of America.

Introduction

Hello, my name is Earl Phelps and I have been drawing for many years. It was my first time starting school that I can recall picking up a pencil and drawing. My kindergarten teacher drew a picture of an elephant and had everyone in the classroom copy it, I have been drawing ever since.

At the age of nine I became interested in supercharacter comic books. I was never a comic book collector, I say this because I would buy a book on the merit of the artwork rather than the character(s) or storyline of the book. I drew the characters of books I bought from stores, but after awhile I started creating and drawing my own supercharacters, it was more fun.

The costume characters in this book have no names and are only created as idea-helpers for you. I made this book for all of those who are interested in learning how to draw and create their own supercharacters and those who are already doing so. If only I could have had a book like this when I was growing up, it would have made it much easier for me in learning how to draw.

This book has very few words because the illustrations speaks for themselves. This was done to induce you to pick up a pencil and start drawing. The only way you can learn how to draw is to draw, and that is the purpose of this book to implement practice, practice and more practice in learning how to draw your own *Supercharacters*.

                                                Earl R. Phelps
                                                Cleveland, Ohio

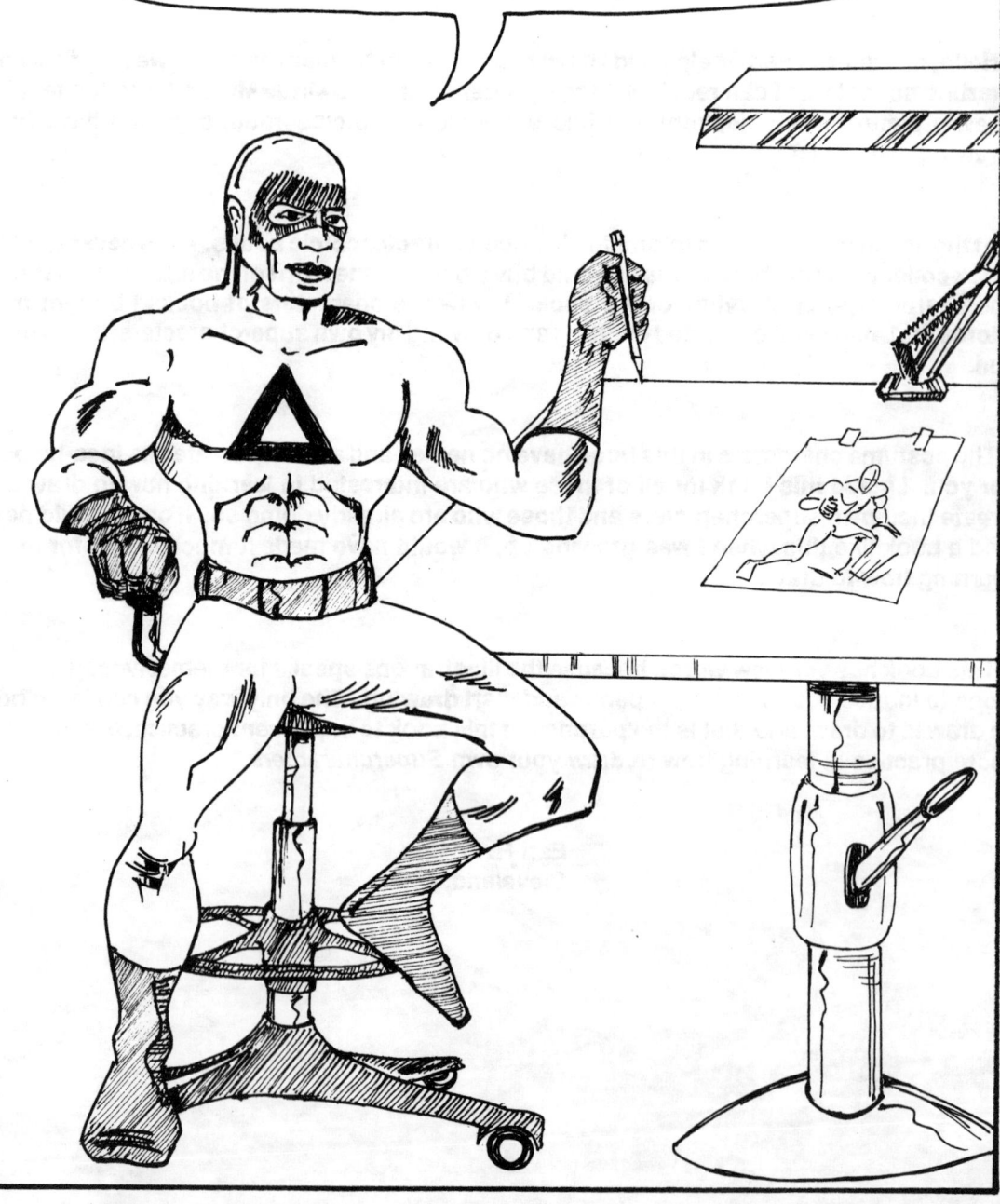

LOOSEN-UP EXERCISE

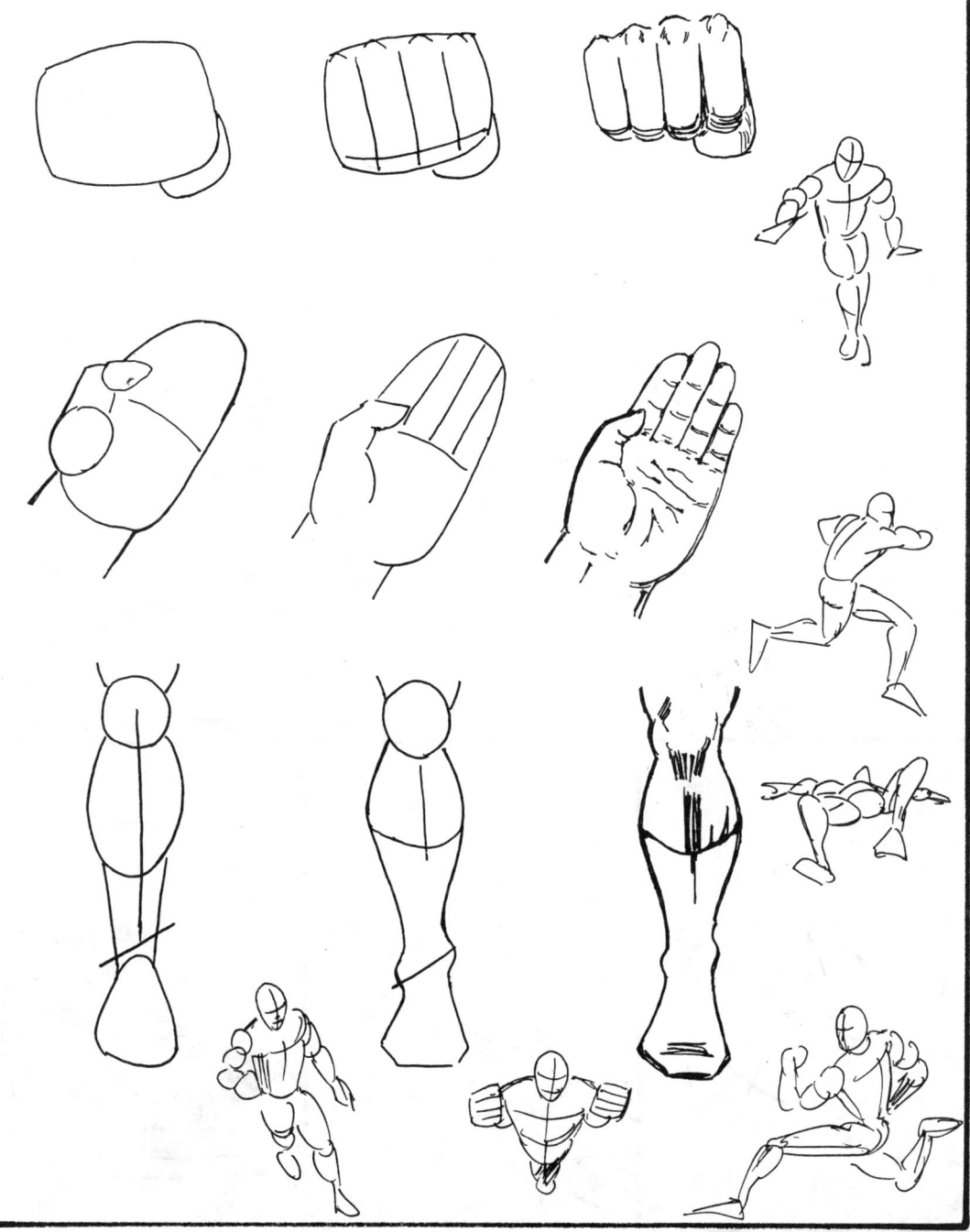

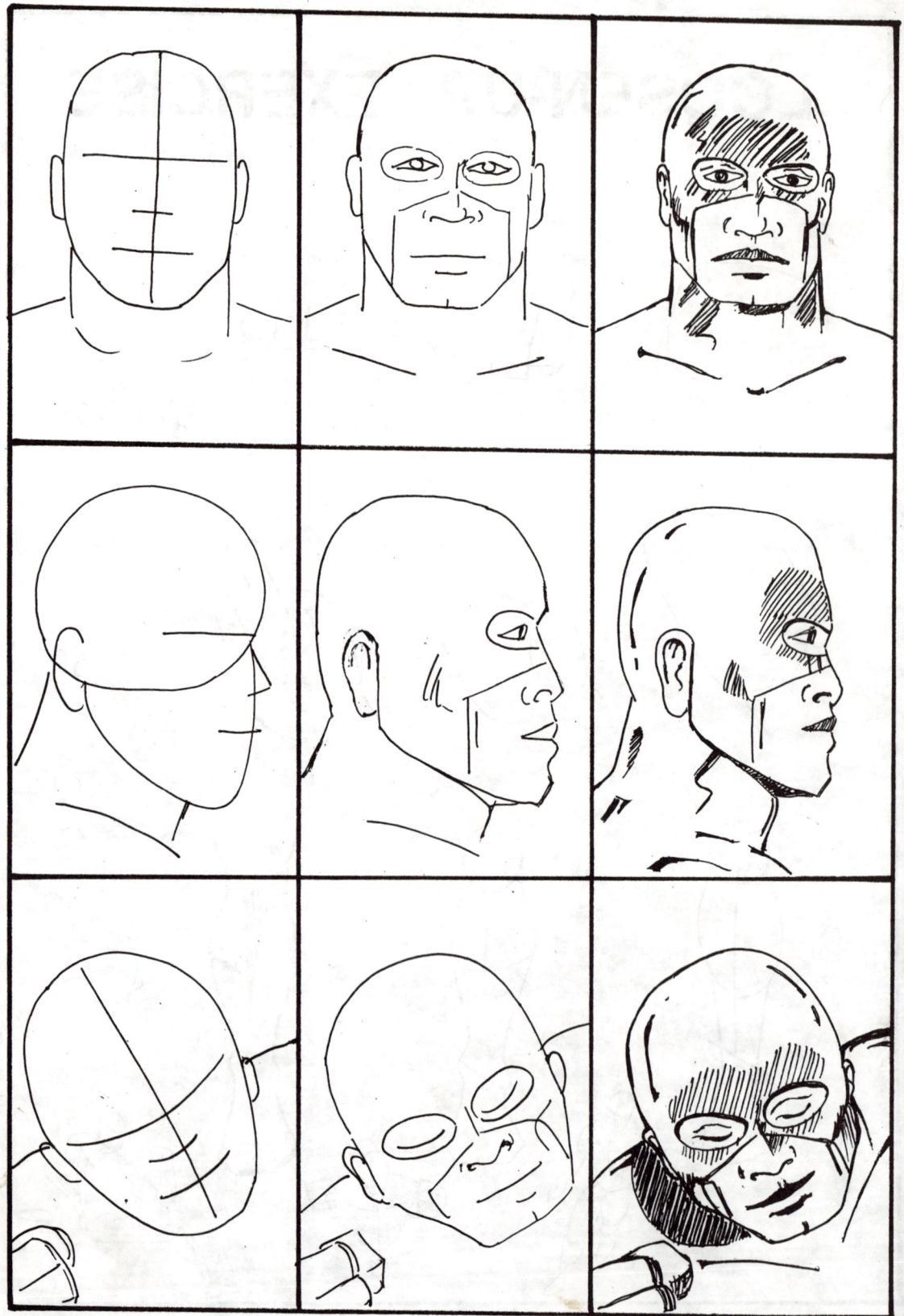

FACIAL EXPRESSIONS

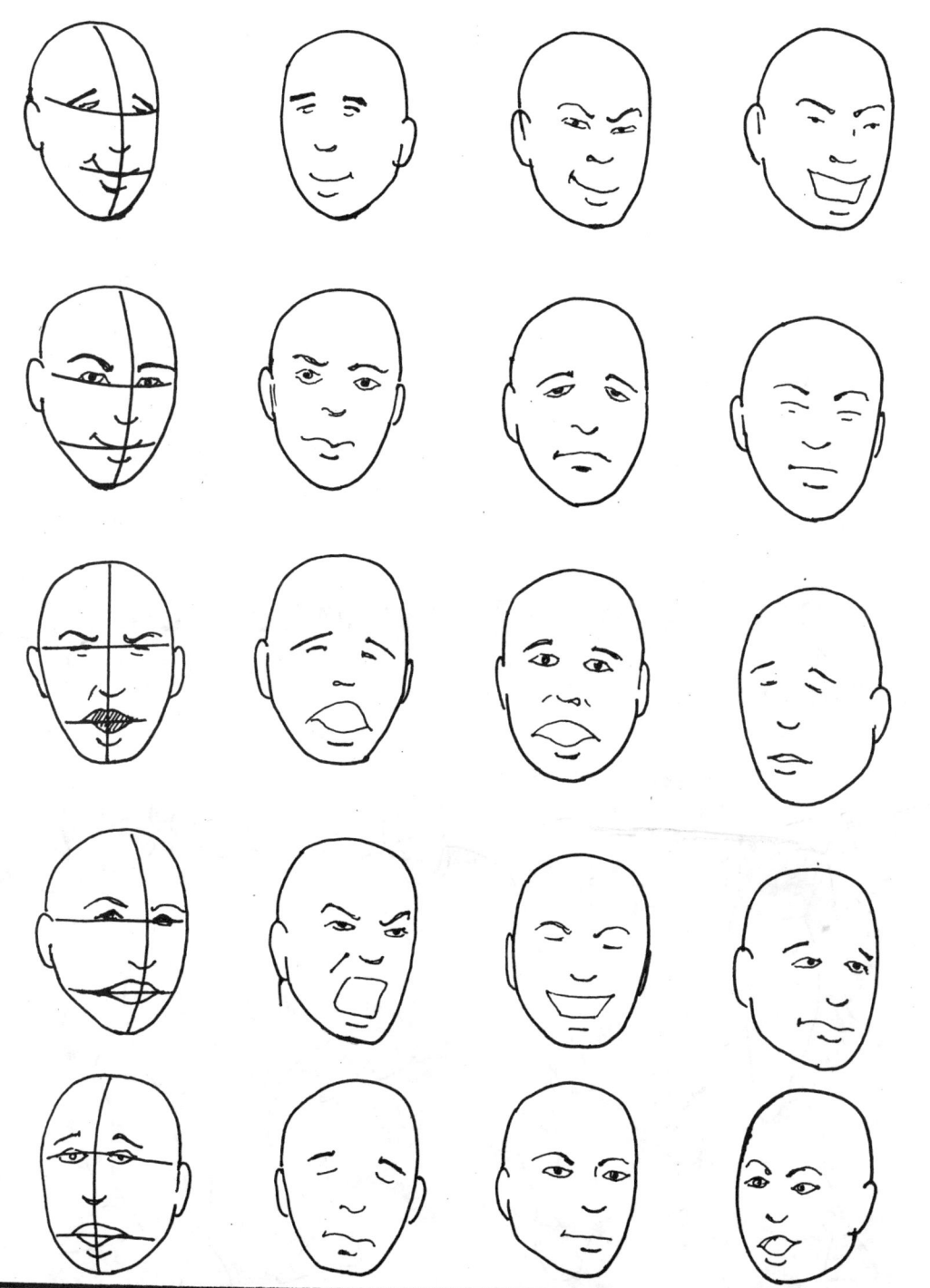

Some like to start drawing human forms from Stix figures. I don't.....

.....It is best to start drawing from forms.

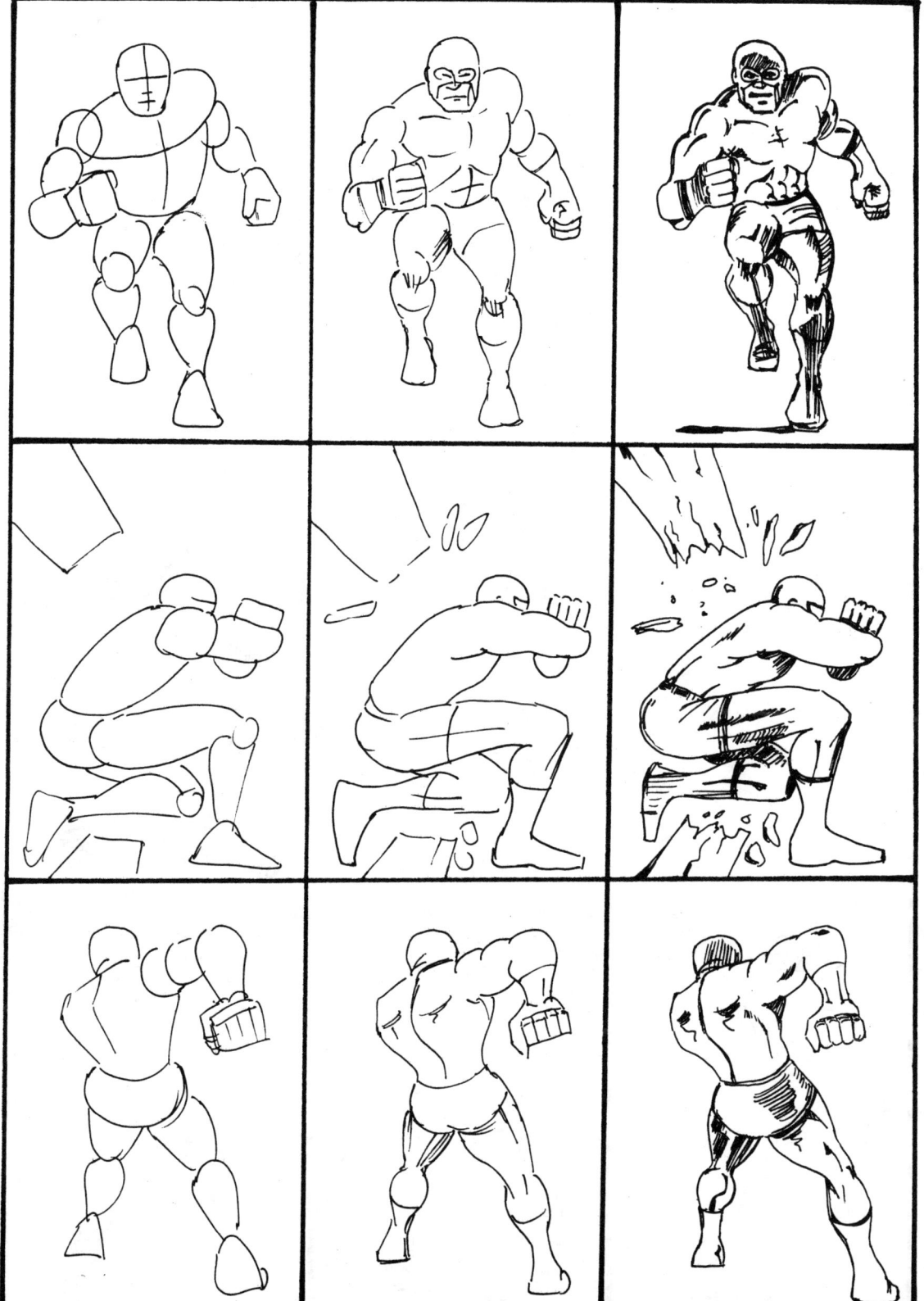

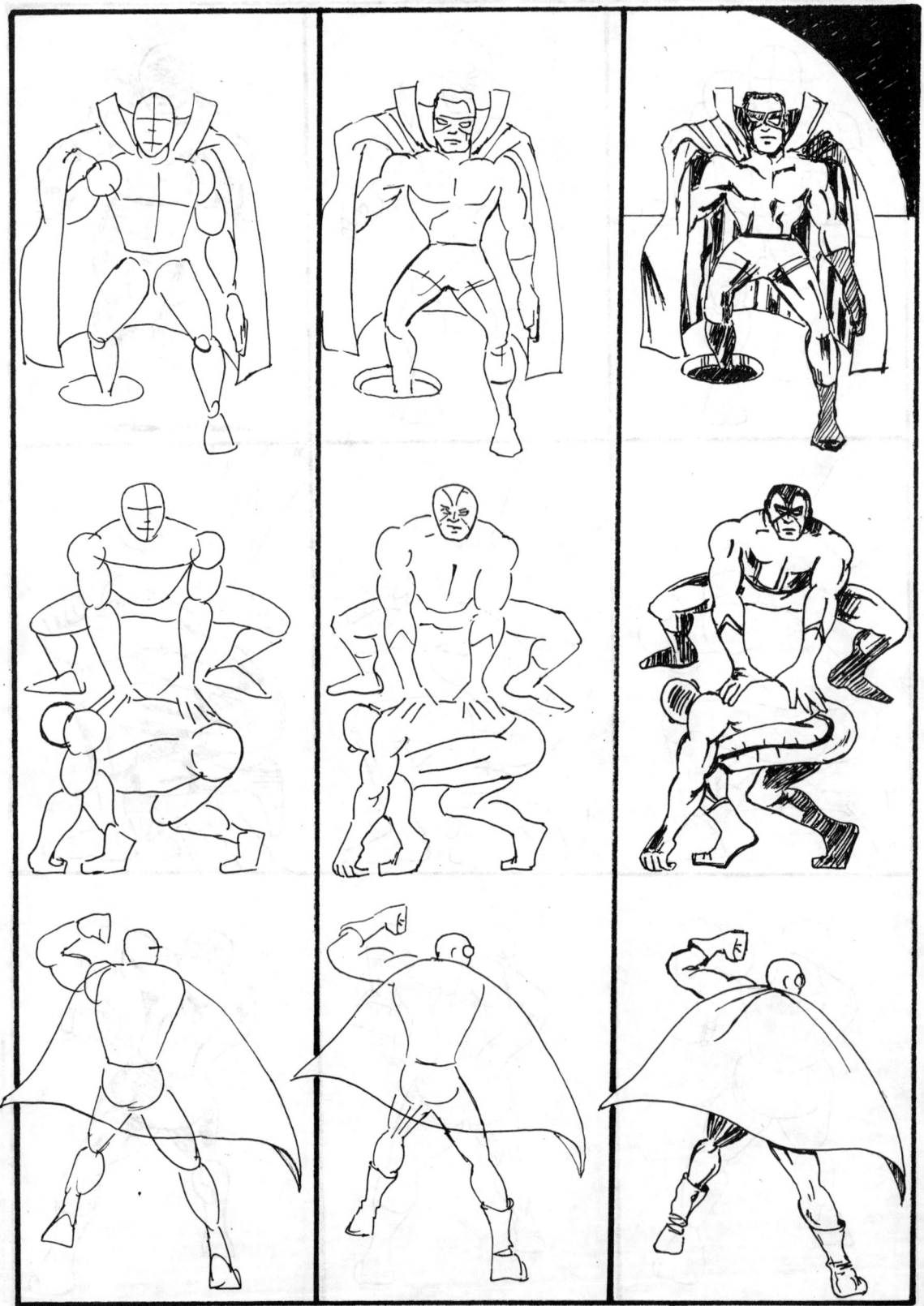

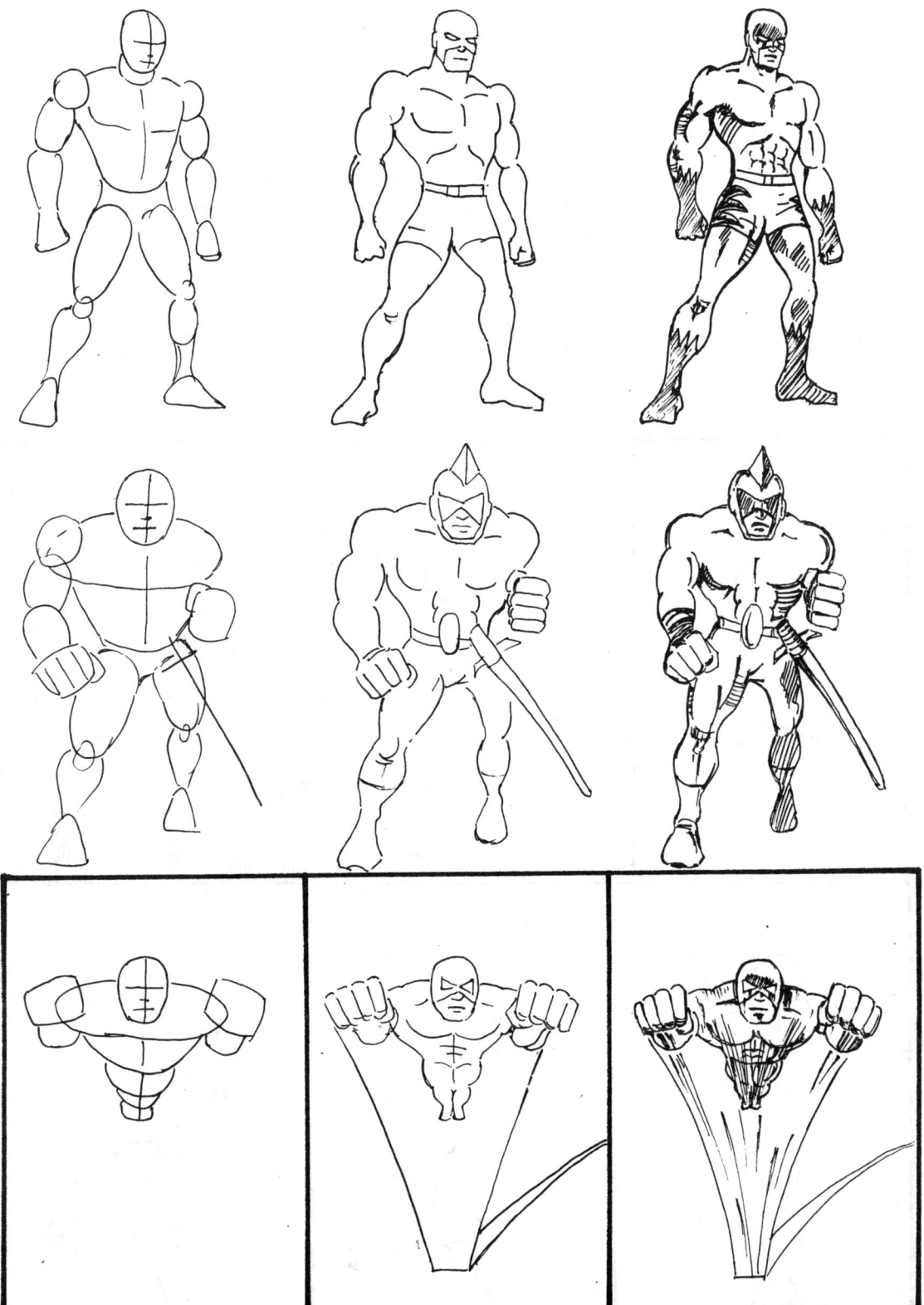

Let's Loosen-Up Again, just relax and start scribbling.

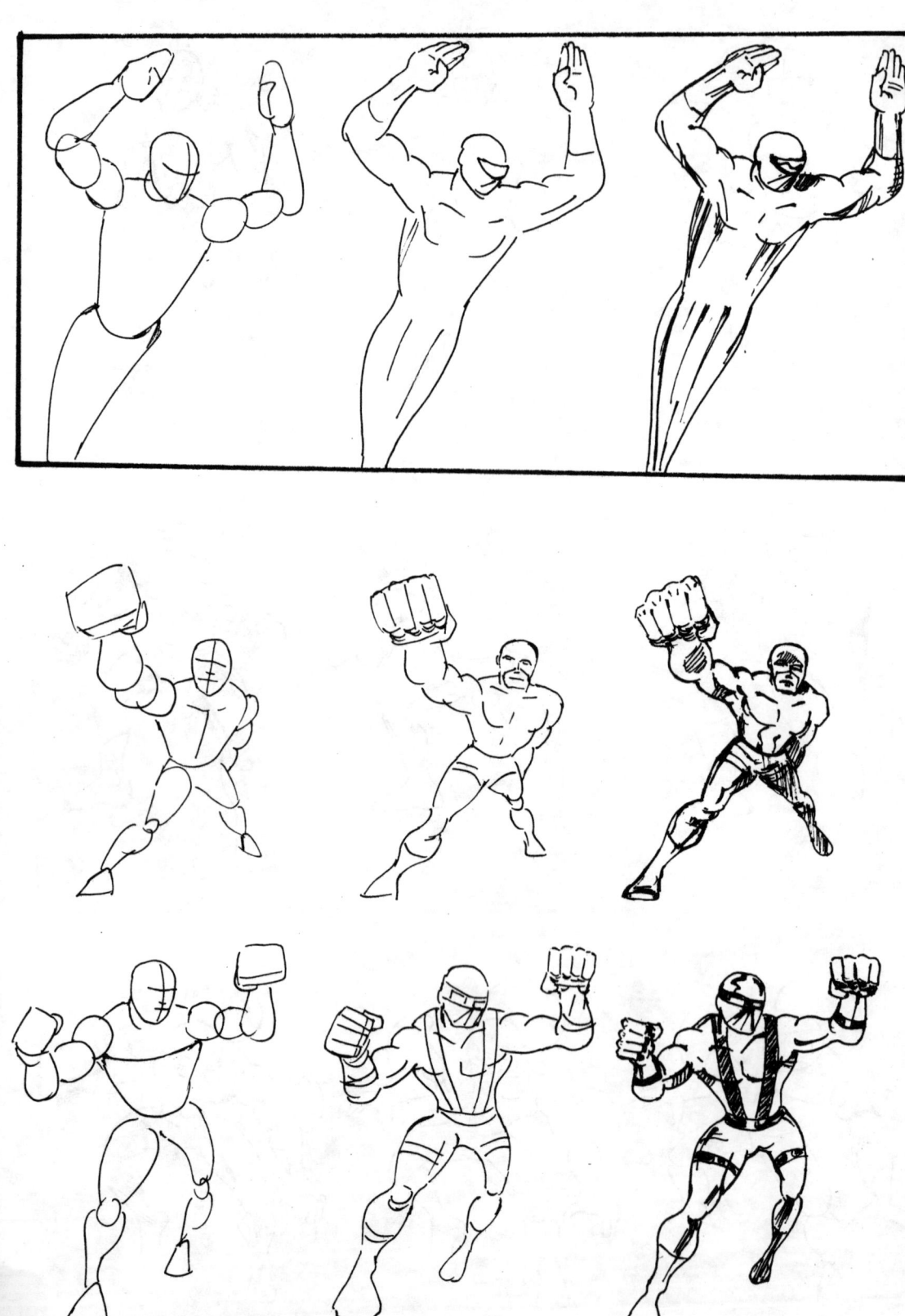

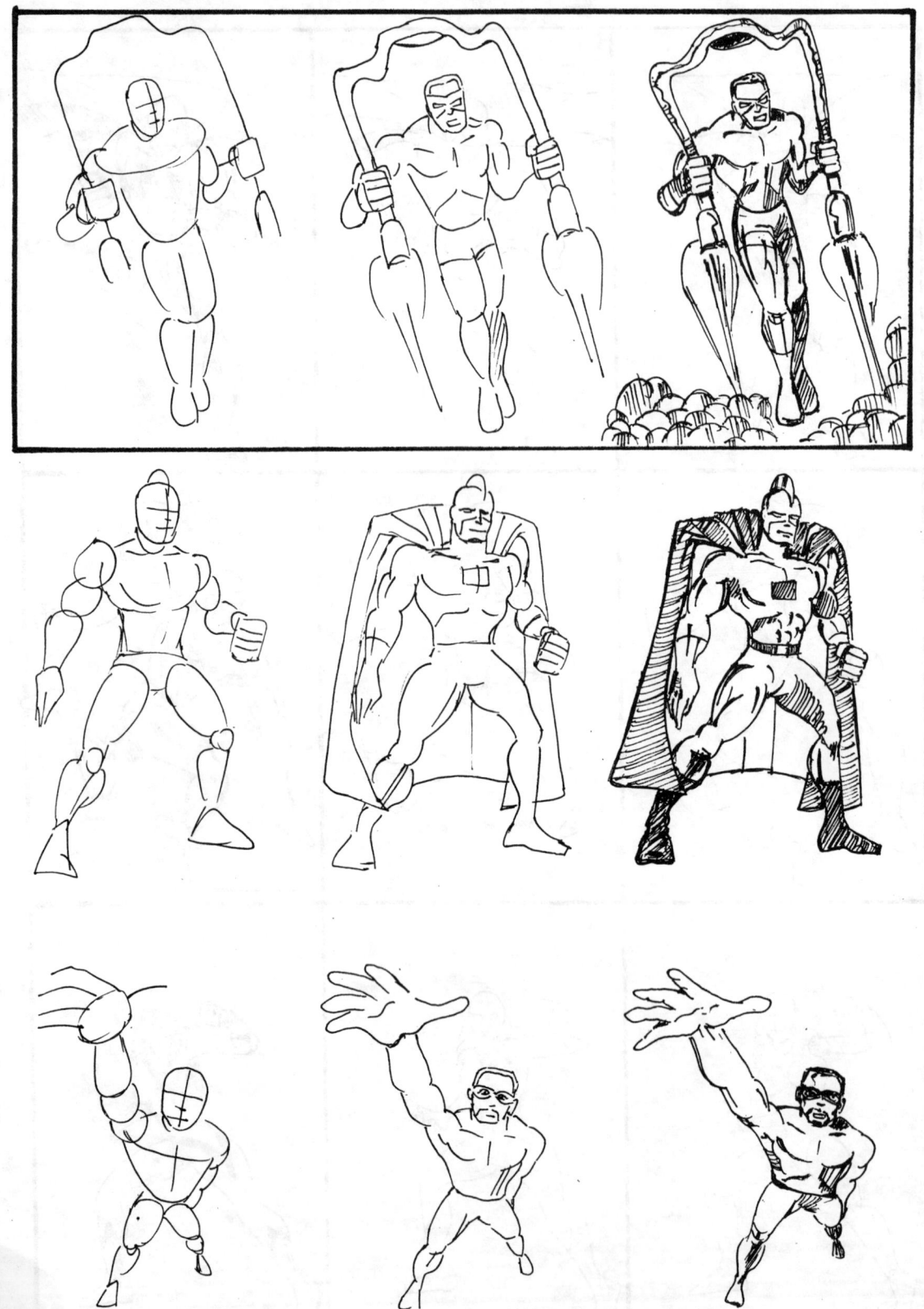

Construct the Drawings below in forms (as I have done throughout this book), and bring it to a complete finish as it is below.

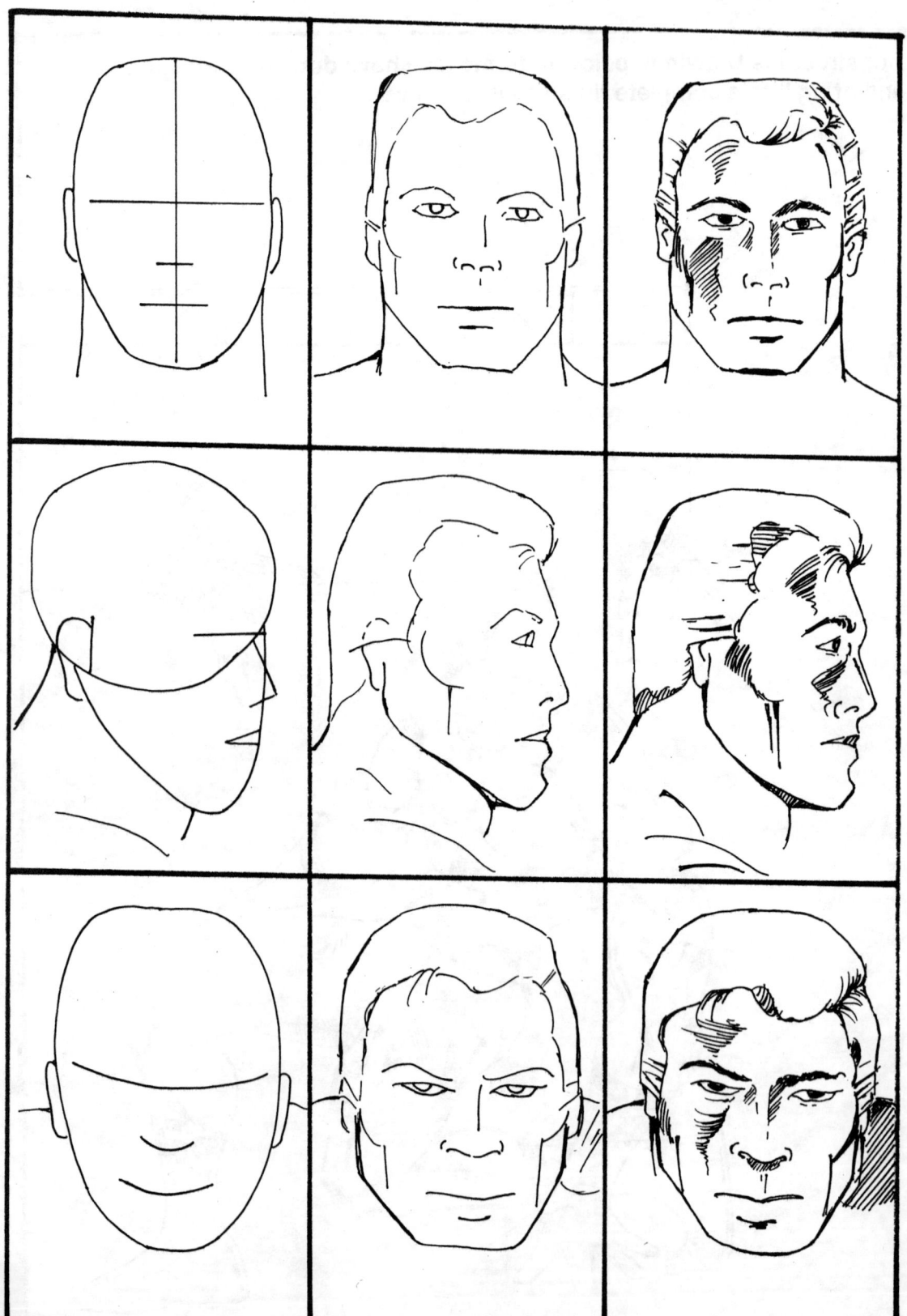

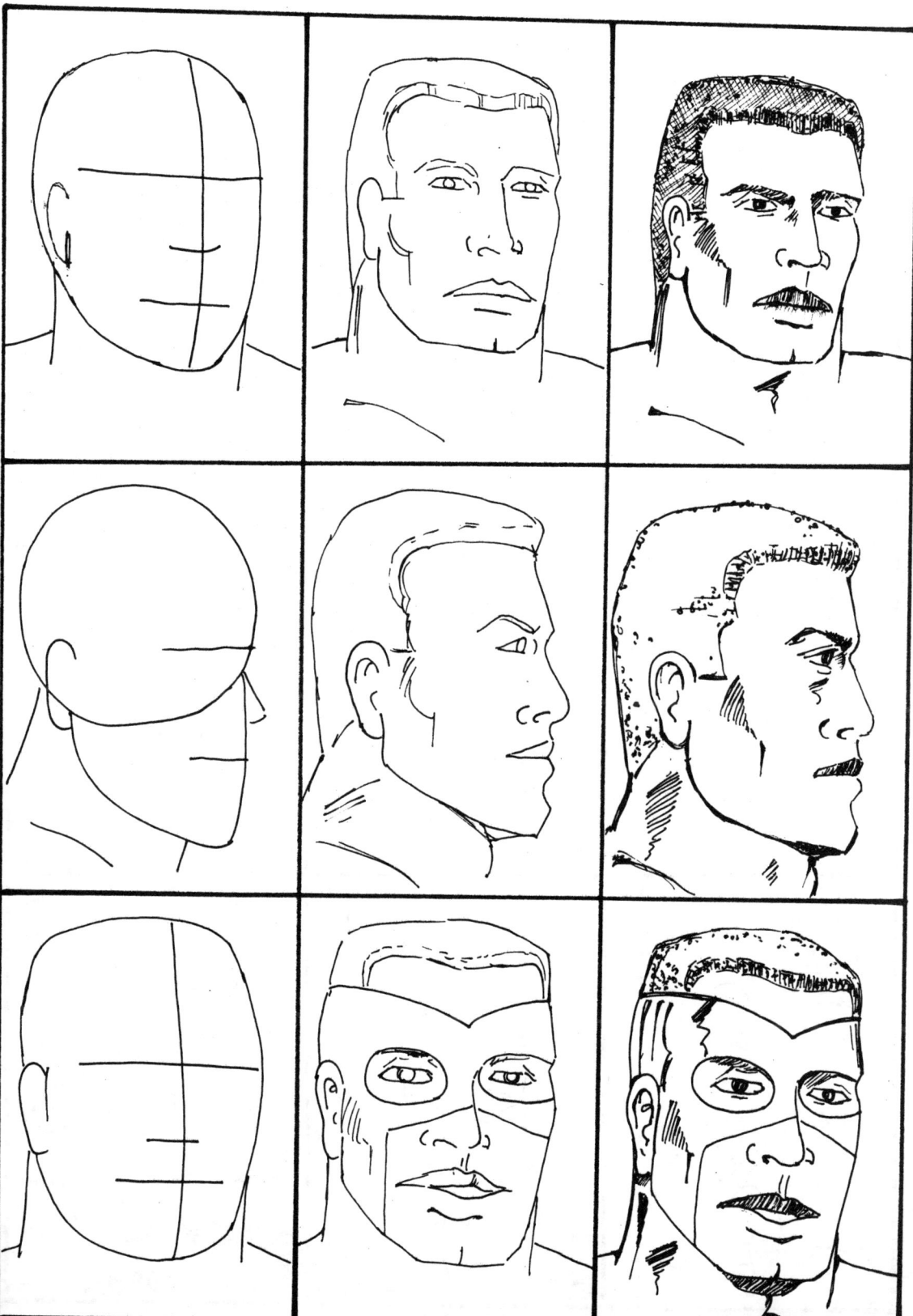

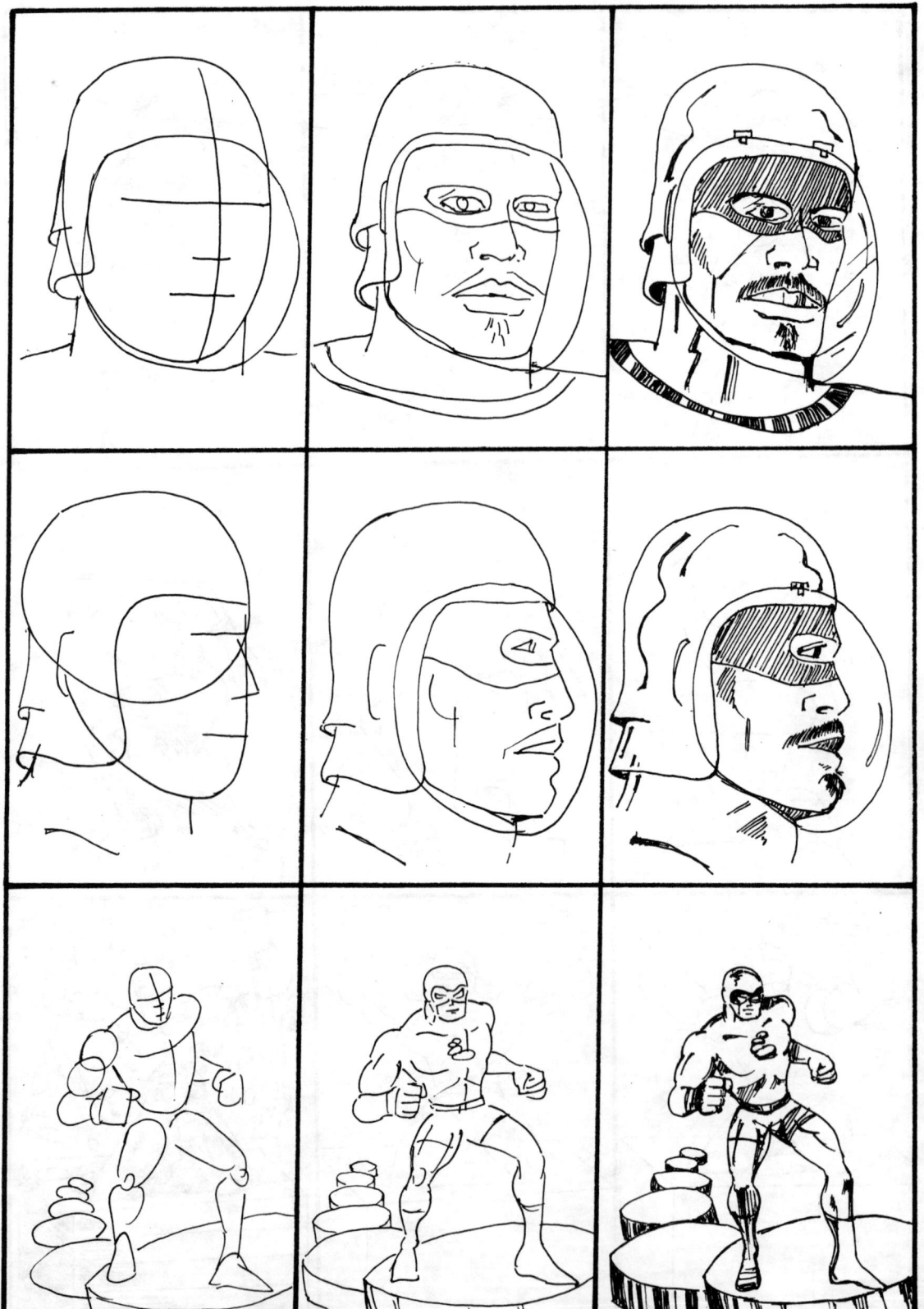

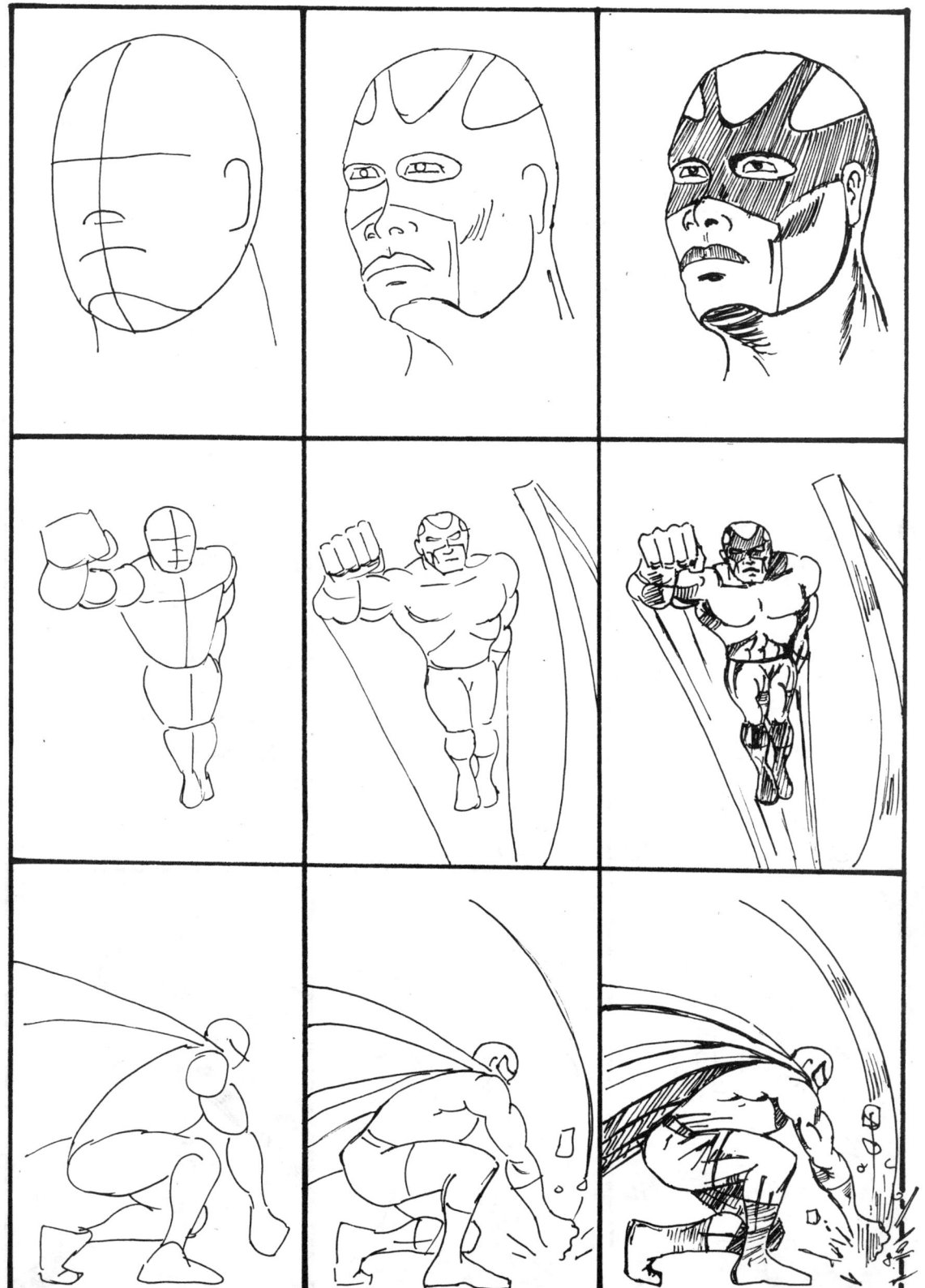

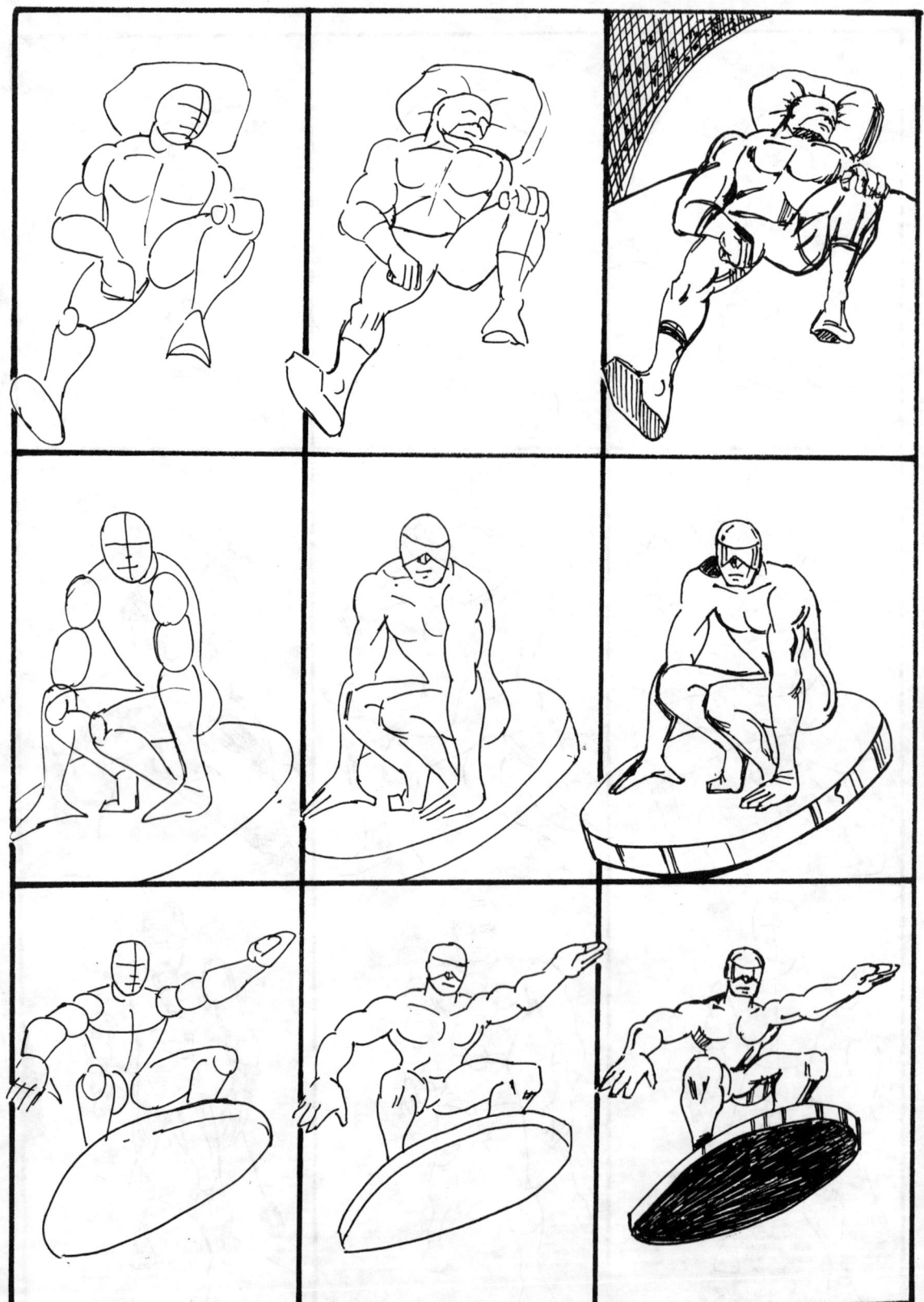

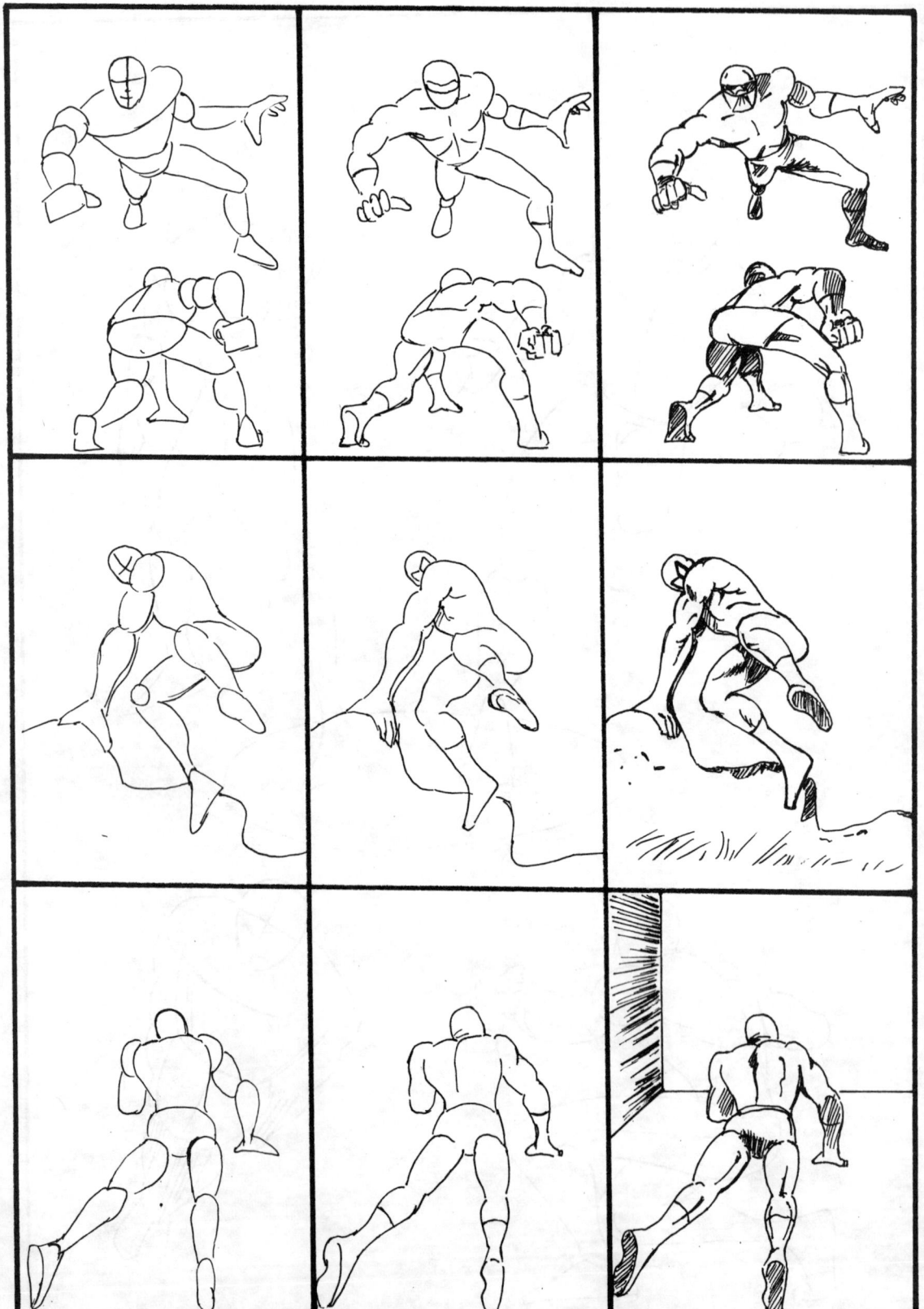

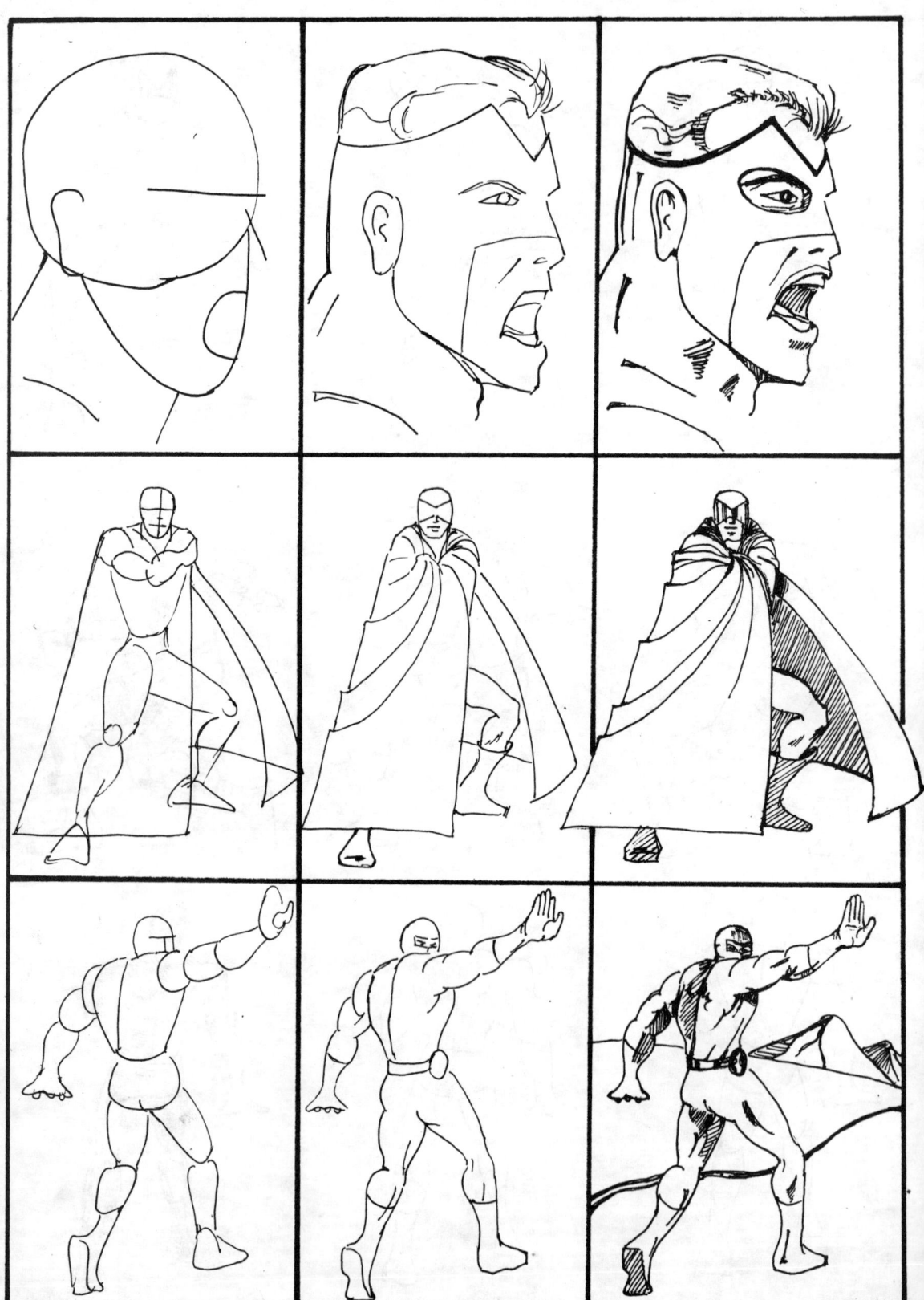